Dedicated to every dream that has yet to take flight...

Onward and Upward

Jenna Harwell

Self-published
2014

Introduction:

I think there is something significant to be said about the changing of the seasons. As summer fades into fall, it brings crisp air, golden leaves, and pumpkin spice lattes. It's a gentle kind of change that you might miss if you're not paying close attention. From day to day, there isn't much change, but ever so slowly, everything is different. In the same way, our seasons in life drift into one another. Sometimes there's a marked difference from one season to the next. Maybe it's with a certificate, or a celebration, somehow the world acknowledges this new change and you accept it as you phase into the next, new, grown-up version of yourself. In my twenty-two years I've accumulated many marked seasons in my life: high school, YoungLife, cross-country, Harding, Camp War Eagle, K-State, Ireland. I've worn many labels: Christian, daughter, sister, friend, student, mentor, mentee, acquaintance. Some experiences have overlapped, some labels complement each other, and some belong to completely different walks of life. They were seasons, and they were beautiful.

To embrace my current season, that of a college student, I wanted to be fully present. All too often, we float through life, waiting for the next big thing to happen and forget that there's so much life already happening in the present. The day it hit me that I was leaving Manhattan, Kansas I wanted to sit down and collect my thoughts. I wanted to be introspective and dig a little deeper into the season of senior year. This book is simply a collection of essays. It's just my thoughts on life, a recollection of my experiences, advice that I've lived by, and encouragement I hope will lighten your day. If you're reading this, you've probably had a large impact on who I have become today. I have been blessed by a wonderful community, full of loving family and friends. I am who I am today because of those people who have invested in me and helped shape me into the best version of myself I could choose to be.

So, this is dedicated to you. To all you who have woken up early to catch the sunrise, you who have poured me a cup of tea, and blessed me with words of truth and affirmation. All who have stayed at coffee shops with me for hours, ran countless miles, and you who have led me when I was at a cross-roads. Thank you. Thank you for investing in me and doing life with me. I hope that you can identify with some of my passages, no matter what phase of life you're going through. I hope that it resonates well with your soul. This is dedicated to all those still chasing the light, spreading love, and experiencing life to its fullest.

Nourish What You Already Have:

"Wherever you are, be all there."
-Jim Elliot

As I enter my last year of college, I am only graced with one certainty: I will be leaving Manhattan come May. Other than that, my future is so unwritten. With that certainty lies a few options of how to live. I can either lust after my cap and gown, setting my sites on a date set in stone. Or, I can continue to live day by day and invest well in my community. The answer might be obvious upon first glance, but the reality of it is that it's hard to put time and effort into something that will gently fade away. A lot of times when we're presented with the ending of a story, that's the only thing we can view it as. Just an ending and the call to end our investments along with it. This year, I'm going to try to evade that trap. I'm going to try with all my might to keep on investing, to keep on nourishing.

I first came up with the goal to "nourish what I already have" when I was about to take flight to a summer in Ireland. I noticed that I was only half present; part of my mind was in Kansas while the other portion was overseas with my future. When I recognized that deep desire within to be somewhere else, I went through my life and wrote down the blessings that were sprinkled in my present. I saw that even though my prayers about the future were being so certainly answered, so were the ones in the present. Even though I was only in a college town in Kansas and not a whimsical city in Ireland, there was still plenty of whimsy here in Manhattan. So I decided to nourish, and that's when all the greatness began...

I found my niche in a lot of areas. My church, my sorority, my classes, my family, my friends. Those areas needed me at my full capacity, not just a visit when I was back from daydreaming. It was a slow process, but it prepared me for today and all of the adventures that go along with the last year of college. Whenever you find yourself longing after a distant date in the future, remember to nourish. Plant good seeds where you are and stay a while to help them grow. If it's a wedding you're planning, remember to soak up the time that you're engaged. If it's a future career that you know you're going to succeed at, remember you are still called to work your hardest at your present job. And if you're moving to a new a city, remember to visit your favorite places often and live fully where you reside. Bloom where you are planted.

Set God Sized Goals:

No matter how young or old you are, how new or experienced you may be, you can always find a thousand excuses for why you shouldn't do something. When you think it'd be neat to go backpacking in Europe, you can find figures to show that you don't have enough money for such an endeavor. When you want to speak up, your mind will easily show you scenarios that make you seem foolish. The tricky part is not the actual feat; it's having enough faith in your dreams to see them through to culmination.

My friend mailed me a copy of The Lion Chaser's Manifesto a couple years back. It's a simple man's vow to life, a vow that he will not live complacent. The line that struck me most was his vow to set God sized goals. Upon first reading this, I excitedly nodded my head in agreement. I assumed he was just creating another phrase for "dream big." However, after setting some God sized goals, I got to experience the wisdom of truly aiming high.

You see, when we set goals in which we're destined to fail, it makes it so much easier to see His divine intervention. If you ever need a renewal in faith, maybe it's because you've been playing it too safe. If you start being Lord in your life, it's much harder to see miracles. Miracles still happen daily, but instead of giving the glory to God, the glory is kept for ourselves.

What is something you would pursue if you knew you could not fail? Whatever that is, go after it. Whether it's something simple or complex, lean in to God. He will provide for you and bring you to places you could hardly dream up for yourself.

Little Moments:

I've always liked mason jars. They have so many uses: candle holders, sweet tea glasses, canning food, decoration, storage. My favorite usage of mason jars, however, is as a memory bank. I have a jar sitting on my desk labeled "little moments" that I look through often to reflect on and remember how blessed I've been and remember the capacity life holds for being truly amazing. Many chapters in this book were pulled out of that jar as I reflected on how much belly-laughter my life has contained thus far.

The moments in my jar range from broad to specific, short and sweet to quite verbose. Rummaging through today, I thought I would share a few:

Castaway Camp 2008:
YoungLife was a strong flavor of my time in high school. It was an unobtrusive outlet for meeting God with your classmates. It's where I learned how to see Christ in the lives of my friends and family and how to be a Light to the lost and lonely. I was first invited by members of my cross-country team and we soon took over in populating the after school activity. The evening talks were often goofy but would always manage to go in-depth and meet high school students where they needed it the most. The summer after my sophomore year in high school, I had the privilege of taking a twelve hour bus ride with my friends to a summer camp in Minnesota. And it was well worth the drive. The things I learned from Castaway may not have all affected me that day, but I still find myself drawing upon such lessons until this day. It also exposed me to some wonderful authors and musicians that have impacted my taste in literature and music. The reason YoungLife was so impactful in my life was because of how the leaders mentored us so well. They were open and honest about how they had made mistakes in their past. They were perfect examples of how God uses people and their imperfections to greet

us where we need to be met, and lovingly guide us back to the right path. It also provided community within the public school system. It caused accountability and encouragement to flow through the hallways and gave us a fun outlet to just be teenagers.

Riding along the Oregon Trail:
Some nights in college will forever be remembered as the best. The night I traveled the Oregon Trail with some of my friends was certainly one of these nights. The Oregon Trail was of course figurative and a result of a themed date party for my sorority. We went all out: prairie dresses, dinner cooked over an open fire, forging the river. It was a joyous occasion with sweet friends, and we couldn't help but radiate happiness the whole evening. When the party was over, we drove out to Pottawattamie State Park for a group bonfire. That's when I dropped another moment into the Little Moments jar. The more detailed moment reads, "talking about life, looking at the stars, singing with a guitar, soaking up the warmth of friends amidst the blaze of a bonfire." That little piece of paper contained a whole lot of life. Our group reminded me how blessed I am to live in Community. We just soaked up each other's presence and sang songs together around a bonfire at the lake and had a lot of intentional time together. We all went around the fire and described what our perfect day would be like. It was fun seeing everyone's personalities shine through as some would travel with friends while others would stay close to home in their favorite coffee shops (mine included New Zealand, Jack Johnson, star gazing, family, and friends). Among the moments of intentional conversation, there were also moments of piercing silence. The ones where you can practically freeze time and feel the weight of a second. Those are good moments too. I think a lot of times we get caught up in trying to be heard that we forget to listen. But, oh, what a beautiful sound when we are collectively listening, speaking with our hearts as opposed to words.

Cinnamon rolls on Sunday morning:
This memory is not a single moment but a collection of Sunday

mornings that have comprised my life. Ever since I have been able to formulate memories, the Harwell family has indulged in a beautiful tradition: Sunday morning cinnamon rolls. This sweet tradition probably began as a way to bribe my brother and me to get ready for church in the morning. Thankfully it has continued into adulthood when we no longer need bribes. I'm not only thankful for the chance to eat my favorite food once a week, but I'm also thankful for the fact that I was born into a family that taught me the importance of indulging in the good and beautiful things life has to offer. There are so many moments in life that we have the power to make exciting and extraordinary, but sometimes we choose the easier route. My parents could have just poured us a bowl of cereal each Sunday morning growing up and we would have turned out just fine. But choosing to bring cinnamon rolls into our lives enhanced my childhood and made Sunday my favorite day of the week. It's simple, really. When presented with the choice of a normal day, or introducing something unusual or spectacular, choose the latter. It can be something as simple as riding your bike to work, or painting your kitchen bright yellow, or stopping by a fruit stand during a road trip. It can be something as simple as eating cinnamon rolls on Sunday morning.

Be Bold:

Along with Little Moments, many chapters of this book are derived from a little project I started this year called "Word of the Week". Whoever I happen to be with on a Sunday afternoon, I ask them to pick a word that we can work on together. Some words are fun, like "Yes", where we have to say yes to every opportunity within moral boundaries. Others are challenging, like "Discipline", where work comes before play. I have been amazed at how much the words vary from week to week. It's been a great glimpse into the personalities of my friends and family. It's also kept me on my toes, never knowing what new lessons would be woven into the week.

It all began the first week of senior year. My friend Allie was in town visiting before she got swamped with the demands of nursing school. On the porch of our favorite coffee shop, we both came to the realization that we were both lacking in boldness. Since we're both pretty confident and proactive, this came as a surprise. But we came to find there were many areas in our lives that we were simply waiting for things to happen. What just seemed like normal living to both of us was actually just a euphemism for complacency. We wouldn't have it. Instead of going about this challenge alone, we knew we'd be more successful with encouragement from each other. Quotes about being bold were exchanged, we challenged each other to branch out and not settle for comfortable living, and we listened when we just weren't feeling so bold. By the end of the week, boldness came a little bit easier and began to transpire into daily living.

Boldness did not stop after those seven days. Now, when I'm presented with a situation requiring me to step out of my comfort zone or to actively pursue something, I go for it. I reflect upon our week of being bold and remember how we were certainly able. No excuses. So instead of just switching out words each week, the lessons have built upon each other. Each week sees me a little more refined and a little more intentional with the community around me. If you're ever struggling with a certain aspect in your life, grab a friend and ask them to work on it with you. Chances are, they're probably dealing with a similar situation. Being open with those around you only strengthens community. Working together to bring about improvements can bring about so much more than you originally intended. So grab a friend, start being bold today.

Run Like the Wind:

There's something about the wind brushing your face that makes you come alive. Whether it's driving with the windows rolled down, biking down a hill, or simply running, it's a gentle reminder that the world around you has a pulse. And that pulse is beating quickly. I suppose that's why I have an innate desire to run long distances, despite the aches and pains that sometimes accompany. I'd like to say my love of running has always been part of me, just like my love of a gentle summer breeze, but my passion for running snuck up on me slowly.

It was a hot August afternoon; I was fourteen and physically prepared to run two miles. Mentally, I was prepared for even less. The combination of the high summer heat and the low desire to finish what I had started almost led me to quitting on that first day of practice. My lungs felt like the midday sun and my calves blazed just as brightly. It's a miracle I went back to practice the next day, but I am so grateful that I returned. Because that next day, it didn't feel so hot, and I didn't feel so awful. Slowly but surely, I got used to the buildup of miles and the building of friendships. It was there I met my Cross Country Family, a team of brothers and sisters to run side by side through life.

Maybe it was the miles that bonded us, or maybe our common interest in coming alive like the wind, but my teammates quickly became my closest confidantes. Mile after mile, we'd trot through town and become better versions of ourselves. Our coach emphasized discipline, which is a tough virtue to instill during the season of invincible teenage-hood. But Coach taught us all about delayed gratification. We wouldn't improve our race times or endurance without practice. Our physique wouldn't change instantaneously, we needed to gain patience before we'd gain muscle mass.

Graduating from high school didn't mean graduating from the cross country team. My teammates have ran through life with me, and stood by my side when I needed stability most. Upon first glance, this extended family is an odd conglomeration. We're comprised of extraverts and introverts, adventurers and home-bodies, chill and spastic, medical field and education field. But we all have one thing in common, and it's not the love of running. Some of us made it through the four years of competition, while others remained active cheerleaders during the races. No, that one thing wasn't a love of running, but rather a respect for our ability to be able to. We all have bonded over the years of how tough life, like racing, can be. And we've all grown closer through cancer, divorce, abandonment, and broken-hearts. We've grown closer because we learned the importance of perseverance, both on and off the pavement.

A group of people that taught me the most about perseverance were my patients in Ireland. Through my internship, I had the daily pleasure of working with multiple sclerosis patients. This group of patients had a unique set of goals. Instead of striving for complete recovery, they used physical therapy as a means to keep their baseline of physical activity and try not to waiver any further away from their current mobility. Despite loss of muscle movement and control over motor functions, these patients remained optimistic. However, each one admitted how much they craved the normal, healthy life they once lived. These cravings and longings led them to offer me some advice: live to the fullest. Each day, we wake up and assume that our health will be similar to when we fell asleep the evening before. But, I realized I was not guaranteed any more healthy days than any of the patients that sat before me. So instead of concentrating on the sadness that accompanies disease, I let it spur me onward to a healthy life. Working with multiple sclerosis patients rejuvenated my zest for life.

My lungs, they're full of air, not tumors and liquid. My muscles, they respond when my brain signals for movement. Today, I am healthy; tomorrow is still unwritten. I am not promised any cancer-free moments, but here I am without it. So, I will take these healthy lungs and breathe out words of hope and encouragement to all I encounter. And these working muscles, I'll suggest day after day that they adventure. I'll tell my working legs to hike along my favorite trails and run until my heart's content. This is what I'll do with each morning I still wake up healthy. How will you acknowledge your health? Will you bike to school and work? Will you lend a helping hand to those around you? Whatever you choose, always remember that we've been given the divine gift to be human. With that in the back of your mind, it's hard to do anything less than living life to the fullest. So take that sweet knowledge and run towards all that's good and beautiful.

Connectedness:

"What if you're just a vessel/ and God gave you something special/ it ain't yours to throw away/ no, it ain't yours to throw away."
                                        -Sam Palladio (lyrics)

I come from a long line of people watchers. My mom tells me about how she used to get in trouble for staring when she was little because it might come across as rude. Growing up, they'd spend the afternoon at the zoo and she would run out of time to eat because she was too busy watching the interactions around her. Her people-watching tendency was not disciplined away, however. It followed her into adulthood and became an unintentional handed down trait to her children.

My first cognizant recollection of people watching happened in California. We were visiting family and decided to spend the day on the beach. It was a bright beautiful day, seagulls soaring through the air, volleyball tournaments in the sand, families picnicking nearby. And in my little mind, I begin to realize as I glanced around, that they all had a story. Every single one of them had something unique that had happened to them. But here we all were, on a beach together, soaking up the sun together, splashing in the waves together, and we didn't even know each other's names.

From that day on the beach, I have grown to appreciate interactions with strangers. They are fleeting, but they are still meaningful. I know that I will never know the depth of our interactions, but I like to think that every event contains a deeper meaning than meets the eye. We have no idea how saying hello in the park will affect the recipient's day. We have no idea if paying for the toll behind us will spark a trend of paying it forward. We have no idea, but we can sure dream.

While I enjoy conjuring up stories about how one life affects the other, I also like tangible stories that show how vital human interactions are. The students at K-State have a beautiful array of hobbies and interests. While we're all fairly similar, it's fascinating to reflect how we all ended up in the same microcosm of a society. Two seemingly different people, who may never have more than a passing interaction, still belong to the K-State family. When reflecting on the microcosm of K-State as well as our sorority, my friend Anna shed some perspective on it. She said, "We're all just wanderers whose lives lined up for four years." I liked that imagery. How our lives are all paths and they cross lines with others. It may be for an extended period of time like family, or maybe a brief section like college. But then there are also those people who come into your life for a few seconds, their lines barely intersecting.

While interning in Ireland, I was required to bus into neighboring cities to visit my company's smaller clinics. My first day bussing out, I had some complications ensue. I had the digital proof of my ticket, but I didn't have the hard copy so I had to purchase another to get on board. Along with this minor setback, I got lost once I finally arrived in the new city. My first week abroad, and thousands of miles away from home, I was starting to feel the onset of homesickness. As I walked back to the bus stop after a day of hard work, thoughts began to flood my head. Did I make the right choice in interning abroad? Was I ever going to stop getting lost? Would I get to see my family and friends soon? Mainly I just needed another person to talk to, someone to reach out and brighten my day. Seated at the bus stop sat two people who would do just that. I never caught their names, but they were a couple in their seventies that were still just in love as the day they married. I sat down next to them and we laughed about the notoriously tardy public transportation system. The bus was already ten minutes late and the people around us were starting to get anxious. To ward off any future anxiety, my new friends had a sweet suggestion: ice cream. The couple had recently come from the hospital for some tests on the husband's heart. But that day also happened to be their anniversary, so they wanted to ward off the ensuing bad news and the bus delay with sweets, and they invited me to join in on the celebration. They bought me some delicious ice cream from a nearby stand and we melted the next hour away together until the bus finally made an appearance.

I soaked up so much wisdom from this elderly couple. Perhaps the most vital information that has stuck with me was their view on relationships. We had been chatting about their anniversary and how beautiful it was that they got to spend yet another year together, especially with the husband's declining health. A couple generations ahead in both wisdom and experience, they pointed out some pretty scary trends in our generation that I had simply been justifying. It wasn't a rant, but they wanted to teach me how to divorce-proof my marriage and to solidify my friendships. They pointed out that the biggest enemy to any relationship now was the need for instant gratification. We all want the happy feelings that come along with human interactions, but aren't willing to work through the hard parts. When the going gets tough, not only do we throw it away, but we upgrade to the newest version that we've convinced ourselves we need. They told me the cure to this was simple, it was respect. Respect for your spouse, respect for your boss, respect for your friends, and respect for yourself. When you see the value in other people, you are willing to be patient and experience delayed gratification. It is only with respect that love will last a lifetime, a love like theirs that had lasted over fifty years.

It was an hour of sweet frozen treats and even sweeter conversations. Their interaction with me was a two-fold blessing. First, I am forever changed by our conversation. I have seen the importance of treating those around me with respect, and I have seen the danger of instant gratification. Second, without knowing, this couple made me feel at home. In the midst of a chaotic day, they were a gentle reminder to stop and enjoy the sweetness life offers. And all it took was buying a foreign gal some ice cream.

We all have gifts and talents. Some people are great at striking up conversations, while others flourish behind the scenes. Some people are gifted with athletic abilities, while others are better suited with a paintbrush in hand. Some people carry messages of encouragement, while others are better at soothing in a time of anxiety. It's important that we reflect upon our talents and see how we can use them to lift up those around us. Life is not meant to be lived alone, and so much beauty is unveiled through conversations with friends and strangers alike. So what gifts have you been blessed with? How are you going to make your mark along the path of life? When you answer these questions and really reflect on the answer, I hope you also reflect on the fact that we are all connected. We are all here on earth living together, and one person's story has the ability to affect countless others. Do not be afraid of letting others in, buying an ice cream cone for a stranger, saying hello to the person next to you. You never know where it may lead and how much the person on the receiving in will need that interaction. Just like I needed that couple at the bus stop, someone needs you to reach out into their lives today as well.

Yoga:

One of my favorite activities is yoga. I try to start off each morning slowly stretching out and preparing myself for the day. The focus of yoga is multi-faceted. It's not only an exercise to keep you in shape, but it also has spiritual/emotional elements that make your mind more clear and often times happier. Many of these elements can be reflected on aspects that we should develop in our everyday life...

Balance:
Though yoga focuses mainly on physical balance, adopting this concept in your own life can have a huge impact. College has taught me, especially this past year, that balance is the key. I notice a huge difference in my attitude if I'm pouring too much time into one area in my life. Even good things can be considered bad if you are solely focusing on them. Take studying for example. If you spend your whole college-hood at the library or in your dorm-room perfecting your knowledge, what did you really accomplish? You're maybe a little smarter than you would have been if you spent time getting to know people, exercising, going out, growing spiritually, and indulging in your passions. But I don't think a few percentage points on a paper is worth sacrificing those other areas in your life. Each area needs a little nourishment if you want to be a well-rounded person. Finding balance will not be an instantaneous thing. You'll need to stretch yourself (just like in yoga) and see what works for you. You may find what was once perfect balance in one chapter of your life finds you off-kilter in another chapter. That's okay, you just have to take some time and find that balance again, that place where you are comfortable yet growing.

Strength:
Yoga slowly but surely develops strength. It's not as apparent as lifting weights; it's a gentle, subtle strength. This is the type of strength that we need to develop emotionally as well. When you

think about strong people, the first image that may pop into your head are those that can take care of themselves, are calloused and emotionless, and will not waiver in times of trial. I don't know about you, but that type of strength is not as appealing to me. Perhaps it's because I do find those people strong, but more so unstable in their might. That is not a type of strength that will be lasting. We need each other, and we need to rely on each other more importantly. Remember first and foremost that strength comes from God. If He's not the source, then it's not an everlasting strength. It will eventually run out and leave you feeling drained and empty. When I was a camp counselor, one of my seven year olds came up to me and shared this verse "My body and my heart may grow weak. God you give strength to my heart. You are everything I will ever need." Psalm 73:26. I was pretty humbled when she read that to me. God lends His strength through others. Start building heart-level friendships if you haven't already. These are the people who will lend strength when you are feeling weakest without expecting anything in return. Let your strength be gentle, inviting those to find rest in their weariness.

Relaxation:
I practice yoga because it is one of the most relaxing things you can do that is still beneficial. There is no real agenda, it flows gently and the movements can be combined in any way desired. Each time it's a little different from the last. I've loved indulging in sunrise yoga that our recreation center offers. There is a surprising amount of people that show up for it being so early. It's because we all know how much more relaxed we're going to be throughout the rest of our day; at peace with ourselves and those around us and ready for the day to come. I like how slow yoga can be, especially contrasted against the business of our lives. In this fast paced world, I think we often forget how to slow down and enjoy ourselves. Think of something relaxing today and practice it. Is it taking your dog for a walk? Is it curling up by a fire and reading a book? Maybe it's going on a retreat or a float trip down the river. Whatever it is, go do it. You'll be a better person for it, even if it means you have to sacrifice something to fit it into your schedule.

Flexibility:

I am not naturally gifted in flexibility. I had a year of ballet and a year of gymnastics, but that's about the extent of my training. At first it was hard and I never thought I'd be able to move like my graceful instructors. Slowly but surely, I was able to mimic their movements and flexibility soon followed. Flexibility in life triumphs the importance of flexibility in body. Our lives are daily altered by those around us, and in the same way our decisions impact those we encounter. We can only control the choices we make and adapt when necessary. Adaptability is an important skill to adopt if you're going to be sharing in life with others (and hopefully we all are). Plan as we may, who really knows what will happen a week from now? And certainly no one really knows what will ensue within a month's time or a year. You have to be flexible and accommodating to those around you. Know who you are and what you stand for, but be willing to shift when the winds require you to. Instead of viewing alterations to your plans as a bad thing, view them for what they are: plot twists.

Plot Twists:

When you start viewing your life in metaphorical terms, like a story, or a work of art, it's a lot less scary. Whatever metaphor you choose, it makes the big decisions in life seem more like a large brush stroke or a chapter with a little more substance. It also makes the little things a little more fun and colorful than they already are. My favorite view lies along the line of literature. My life is a book, there are many chapters which compromise it, and each day a new sentence is written down, some days even deserve two or three sentences!

Just like a book, life contains all the important structures. There are characters, both protagonists and antagonists, page turning cliff-hangers, plot twists, and an overarching theme. You, of course, are the main character in the story. That's not to say you should live selfishly by any means, but like the protagonist, you are only in control of your own actions. You set goals, and the goals you set provide the true flavor of the book. The book then becomes about how you'll get to that end goal, no matter what obstacles come your way. If you decide that you want to start a non-profit organization, the decisions you make along the way make up the substance of the story before you even reach the main goal. You're in charge of what decisions you make in order to start the company, provide funding along the way, and ultimately how you bring about good for others from those decisions.

Upon first glance, the antagonist is the enemy. This is the person or force of nature that is keeping you from reaching your end goal. In the case of the non-profit company, this could be a CEO from a big company, or simply money. But, I like to define antagonist in different terms. I like to simply define antagonist as the person or force that causes the main character to show their true colors. Thus, an antagonist can be a best friend, a tragic event, or stranger you have a conversation with on the subway. When antagonists are viewed in this light, it makes people that were once seemingly enemies become an essential, uplifting part of your story. When you reflect and see that they are put in your life to make you stand up for what you believe in, they become more of a blessing than an obstacle. Friends and family members that have traits opposite of yours can also be viewed as antagonists. You would never want to part ways with them, but you may grow to appreciate them even more if you view them as someone to project your characteristics. The shyness of your best friend now shows how outgoing you are, the careful planning of your sister shows how spontaneous you like to live life. You need people to share interests with and spur you on to your goal, but you also need those to challenge you and cause you to ultimately reflect on your decisions and intentions.

Setting is one of the first things I notice when I read a story. Even though it's just the background, it sticks out to me because I have to see the big picture before I can understand the details. In my life, setting has become a very important piece of the story. This is because of all that setting entails. When you choose where to do life, you are also choosing the little events that will define and make up your experience. You're choosing the state parks you'll hike in on the weekends, the coffee shops you'll sit at and the people you'll sit at them with. Whether you're choosing where to plant your roots, where to attend college, or where to study abroad, choose wisely. Really think about which setting will help you be the best version of yourself.

A good story never contained a smooth plot for the protagonist. No, the main character has to overcome obstacles, insecurities, and most of all, plot twists. If the character set a goal and achieved it over the next few pages, where would the fun be in that? The character would be flat; obstacles are what make them dynamic. The chapters that provide the most excitement aren't the ones with security and known answers. They're the ones that make the character put their hope in something bigger than themselves. These chapters let the character know how much they can handle, and how blessed they are when they're done with the trials. Upon reflection, everything is understood, though it was hazy walking through the hardships. The plot twists are then seen as a gift from above because it halted the main character from going down a path that wouldn't be so full of life.

Let's start living like main characters. Realize that God has given each and every single one of us the gift of life, and live accordingly. Set God-sized goals, pursue your God-ordained passions, and let yourself be swept up with the excitement of the story. View the hard people in your life as antagonists meant to make you grow. Choose a setting that has adventure woven into its fabric. And, instead of being anxious about things not going our way, let's simply view them as plot twists to our life stories.

Surreal:

"Be in love with your life, every minute of it."
-Jack Kerouac

Some stories cannot be captured. The tip of a pen or punch of a key cannot convey the words correctly. Voices can't describe the color of the sunset, and photos can't capture the joy that permeated the night. These particular stories have to be lived in the moment and treasured while they are happening. We write to taste life twice, but the first bite is always the best.

A particularly uncapturable story happened this spring. It was one of those days when you just might start believing the weather man when he says the warm weather is here to stay. You hesitate to leave the house without a jacket, but convince yourself that sixty degrees is plenty warm. This particular day I found myself working inside all day, riding on the promise of a trail run afterwards. And that's what I thought when I woke up that morning. I thought the day ahead of me held work, a run, grocery shopping, and studying for an exam. Little did I know, only one of those would hold true.

As the clock reached five in the evening, signaling work to be over, my friend Hannah called. She asked if I'd want to hammock with our friend David when I had free time. Delighted at the invitation, I started adapting my tentative evening plans, and said I could for an hour or so. That hour quickly turned into the rest of evening and the adventure had begun.

Having been born in Kansas, I've grown to appreciate the vast beauty of the different landscapes she offers. Though most is flat farmland, there is the cityscape, rolling flint hills, lakes, forests, and much more. I still find myself amazed when I wiggle my toes in the sand at the beach and have to remind myself I'm still in Kansas! This adventure started at Tuttle Creek on the "beach". It was crop burning season so the whole town was laced with the scent of bonfire and glazed over with the smoke of crops past. It gave the whole evening a crisp fall feel and made a simple sunset, simply surreal. Our adventure took us from the beach, to very climbable rock walls, and some trails blooming into their spring clothes. At the end of the trail was a bridge over evaporated water. The water had left and wouldn't return until the next heavy rain, so we knew we only had a limited time to hike down under the bridge. The whole scene felt like a dream: a bone-dry river bed, an age-old bridge, a veil of smoke concealing the approaching dusk. Imagine if you will, but my words will not do it justice.

With all of these unusual factors, we knew that it was a once in a lifetime evening. If we brought friends and loved ones back to that place, it'd be different, and we'd be different as well. We'd soon need a raft to lie under the bridge and talk about life, and we'd need our own bonfire to make the air smell so sweet. So we were all in agreement that this evening was simply a blessing, an invitation to deepen our friendship and explore God's beautiful creation.

The biggest thing I took away from that evening was a beautiful sense of peace. Though at first glance it seemed like just another adventure, it had divine intervention written all over it. God decided to save me from an evening of mediocrity. I had enough food to put off grocery shopping for another day, and the exam could still be studied for at another time. So I got to thinking, if God can mold these five hours of my life, how much more can he change five years? I'm on the cusp of some major life changes, but I know with Him guiding, I can continue warding off a mundane life. I had no way of foreseeing that adventure, it was spontaneous, unplanned, and surreal. I just have to keep faith knowing the adjectives of that evening will be magnified into this next chapter of life.

Plans:

When I was ten years old, our teacher gave us an assignment that required much abstract thinking. For our creative writing unit, we were asked to write a letter to ourselves predicting what life would be like in twenty years. To a ten year old, that is quite simply forever away. She told us to think about what kind of career we'd be in the midst of, how many children we would have, what car we would drive, where we would be living, and all the little details in between. My plan went a little something like this...at the age of thirty I would be a high class fashion designer living in a big city. But not just any fashion designer, no, yours truly would be the sole creative mind behind the exquisite line of Limited Too clothing. I would have a home in the suburbs that reflected my fashion choice (think neon and sparkles) and I would tote my children around the city in a Range Rover. If you know the twenty-year old version of me, you know that those predictions are about as polar opposite as could be. I'm living in the half-way mark between writing and receiving that letter, and I am extremely grateful that my path has been slightly altered.

I'm not mad or disappointed that thus far my life has turned out different than I predicted. I'm sure if I sat down and had a chat with my ten-year-old self, she'd be able to see that the path I'm on today has just as much whimsy and adventure that I longed for in those days. She'd be able to see that different doesn't always mean disaster. I don't know about you, but I'm still in need of that reminder today. I need the reminder that when plans don't go my way, it's usually because God has something better in store.

As I approach graduation, I can't help but go back to my ten-year-old tendencies and plan out my future. Where will I be in ten years? I'll be a physical therapist, living in a big city, driving my kids around in a Range Rover. Well, we'll just see. Because this year I've learned something very important. God does not have a back-up plan, He has

THE plan. And He has invited me to partake in that plan, and He's promised to weave in all sorts of adventure and whimsy.

In the past month, I've heard three different sermons on Abraham's faith. I don't know if God's trying to tell me something or not, but I'm just going to assume He is. Right now, as I play the waiting game, practicing patience as I am waitlisted at two very different graduate schools, He is teaching me a plethora of lessons. In each of the sermons, it has been pointed out that Abraham didn't even have a direction when God called Him to do great things. He simply told him to pick up his things and go where the Lord called him. Each day, God still calls each and every one of us on a journey. My response is usually, "Absolutely! But before I follow You, I need a detailed list of where I am going, who will be there when I arrive, what my schedule will be like each day, and how this is going to affect my life positively." I'm working on letting my yes simply be yes. I'm working on following Abraham's example of faith and just going.

God only has THE plan, because He is the only one able to see throughout time. He knows the end results before something has even transpired. Living in a linear dimension, we can only live forward and understand looking backward. It makes for being really lousy predictors of the future. That's why God calls us to follow Him and follow His plan, to simply go and trust in His inherent goodness. We can map out our lives and try to predict the twists and turns, but each day it usually changes by lunch time, sometimes even earlier. God doesn't call us to lives different than our own plans just to upset us or show His power. No, He calls us to lives of magnificence because His ability to dream is so much grander than our own. He lovingly says, "Darling, dream bigger. Your plans are good, but mine for your life are great. Instead of fretting about your future, remember that I've got this. Remember that my goodness will always triumph. My plans will always flourish and cause you a life of abundance."

These truths are the reasons I'm starting to reconsider my plans. I'm still graduating in a few months, and I still don't know what life holds for me afterwards. That hasn't changed. What has changed is my release of control. I'm handing over my reservations, my back up plans, my future, and trading them in for faith. An unshakeable faith that's based on trusting in Him and His timing.

Gypsy Souls:

July 25th, 2013 will forever be one of my favorite days in history. It was a simple day, but full of extraordinary encounters. I was in Ireland, winding down for the summer and preparing to head back to the States. My last week abroad, I decided to visit all of my favorite places that I had discovered over the summer. This particular day found me at a café up the hill from my house, sipping on a cappuccino and journaling about my summer adventures. The journal I kept turned out to be a double blessing. Not only was I able to document my trip and taste life twice, but it also served as a conversation piece with strangers. Though Ireland lacks many of the typical social barriers, having my journal out broke down anything left inhibiting conversations with complete strangers. Irish, American, Italian, all approached me when I was journaling. My favorite visitors, however, waited until the last weekend to walk into my life.

Their names were Mary and Georgia, they were seven and eight years old and enjoying a beautiful day in the sunshine. They'd been wandering around the nearby stores and stopped in to get some cake from the cafe. While I was writing in my journal, they approached me with an exclamation of wonder. "What are you *doing*? Are you *writing*? What are you writing *about*?" Georgia inquired in one breath. I told my little friends that I was from America and I was just writing about my time in Ireland. They were more intrigued than any second graders I've ever encountered and it was both endearing and a little worrisome. After a few more minutes conversing, I came to understand that these weren't just two children gallivanting on a parentless-day. They were gypsy children, and my life got a little more magical with their encounter.

It turned out that Mary and Georgia were cousins and both came from large families. Mary had eight siblings and Georgia already had eleven other siblings. Their parents were aloof and probably back with the rest of the colony on the outskirts of town. There's a subculture gypsy group in Ireland and the United Kingdom called The Travelers. It's a rough, nomadic group that have a slightly frowned upon reputation. They are known for being trashy, dirty, provocative, lacking in education, quick to fight, and many people have prejudices against them. Earlier in my summer adventure, I had met a woman who volunteered as an after school tutor for the gypsy colonies. Many children drop out of school at a young age or are forced to by their families due to packing up and moving or social obligations like marriage. She explained that many of the children are bright and quick learners, but the pressure from their families and the need to pursue tradition usually triumphs education. After learning about this culture, I'd been secretly hoping for an encounter of some sort.

The girls pulled up two chairs next to me and we spent the next few hours learning about each other's cultures, favorite things in life, and simply enjoying one another's company. Georgia was the more outspoken of the two and was already developing a chip on her shoulder. A sweet girl, she could not understand why others looked down on her and thought her to be "dirty". Mary had a gentler outlook on life and saw many possibilities where Georgia saw road blocks. In a culture that forces you to grow up a bit too fast, the girls were already focused on tasks that should be saved for a later season in life. Their worries ranged from how they were going to look after their little siblings, how they were going to go back to college after they had married and had children of their own, how they were going to be a doctor or nurse someday. Both had such nurturing spirits and had come to love helping others. Mary decided she wanted to be a doctor and would stay in school, even if her parents wouldn't allow it. Georgia wanted to become a home-stay nurse so that she could take care of people and get to see them where they felt most comfortable. I ripped out two sheets in my journal and drew matching dream catchers for them. On the picture I wrote "Life is a dream, you are a dream catcher." I explained to them that their dreams were important and they had every right to pursue them. It didn't matter where they came from, each day presents them with the option to move towards their goals. They have each other and they have a drive to succeed. We eventually had to part ways, because moments like that sadly can't last forever. But I carry both of them with me in my heart, and I hope someday to hear about them changing their little corner of the world.

My day with the gypsies taught me a plethora of lessons. I had always admired the ramblers, the wanderers, those who spread their wings and fly. I still do, but I came to realize the importance of having both wings *and* roots. The girls expressed their longing for a place to call home for more than a few months, a place that they could grow and develop friendships and attachments. Wings allow us to see places we thought only existed in our dreams. They allow us to go confidently in the direction of the life we imagine and see it through to existence. Roots, however, are the driving force behind our wings. They are the wind, the map, the comfort, and courage behind every journey. They give our adventures substance and they are so necessary and so beautiful.

Mountain Peaks:

Metaphorical Conversations with God: The Leap.

Lord, I've been so busy climbing mountains this year, focusing on the task at hand, that I forgot what I was climbing for. With each step, I've been craving oxygen, but You've said, "Patience child, do not be anxious." As I reached upward to pull myself higher, I craved strength, but You said, "Sweet one, my strength is sufficient for you." And when my head spun and I looked for some sign of direction, the midday sun, the North Star at night, even the shadows exaggerating crevices, You said, "Darling, I am the only map or compass you'll ever need. I am the Way, the Truth, and the Light." So I kept climbing, filled with contentment because I had learned to lean into You, and not on my own understanding. I had learned to climb the mountain with my hands wide open.

When I reached the top, I stopped to look at the view, Your works spread wider than my eyes could see. My stomach leapt as I saw just how far I'd actually come, and I swore to myself that this was the grandest of all human experiences. Life on the mountain peak, with my Savior, holding on to an accumulation of courage, humility, and wisdom. I leaned my head against the rocks and slid down to sit upon the floor of my new home, ready to defend the honor of my newly achieved dream. And as I gazed at the horizon in the distance, the corner of my lips turned upward and I gently shook my head and laughed. Because that's when I realized Your great capacity for working in multifaceted ways. As I was distracted by the climbing and found myself chanting, "Upward, upward, upward," You were working on my heart ever so gracefully encouraging, "Onward, onward, onward."

As I stood up, the blood rushed to my head and I stumbled dauntlessly to the edge. Every fiber in my being wanted to cling to solid ground, but You did not create me for a life of stability. You created me to fly. I looked at my toes, my shoes worn down from the hike. Below them, I saw tiny dots that must be trees, though they look more like ants from this height. I took a deep breath: inhale, exhale, inhale, gulp, exhale. After some reservations, I felt a warmth flow through my veins as you whispered one last time, "My child, it's time to take the leap of faith. Trust that I am God and I am good and I am capable of more than you could ever begin to fathom. I will lift you up on wings like eagles, and take you to places you'd never be able to reach if your feet were securely fastened to this earth. So go ahead, little bird, this is where all the greatness begins." I took in one last breath as I nodded my head, and without hesitation, I took the leap. And a funny thing began to happen, I started to fly…

Contentment:

"If I find in myself desires which nothing in the world can satisfy, the only logical explanation is that I was made for another world."
- C.S. Lewis

An unmet challenge bequeathed an extra dose of humility in my life. The challenge: contentment, the obstacle: life. The carefully chosen word of the week, contentment, was decided after chatting with one of my friends one Sunday afternoon. We were sipping tea on her side porch, warding off the chilly breeze with some steamy liquid. Through our conversation, it was discovered that both of us could stand to work on contentment. After all, we were both seniors lacking direction. That lack of direction was bringing up insecurities that we assumed had been buried the last time we were seniors, in high school. So we challenged each other to an intentional week of contentment. Her struggle with approval in friendships and my struggle with an unforeseen future would surely dismantle after a week. This place of pure contentment seemed so tangible, we even put a definition to it. We decided contentment was not merely peace or joy alone, but the intertwining of the two characteristics. We were ready to set the flavor for the week.

Seven days passed, and I surely didn't feel any more content than when we started this challenge. Personally, I had been focusing my time and energy on a week full of back to back exams. I had been concentrating on these tests to distract myself from the bigger problem, I still didn't know what I was doing after graduation. Would these tests even matter in a few months? I neither succeeded nor lost in the battle for contentment. I merely walked unscathed along the edge of the battlefield. My friend on the other-hand was facing it full on. She was in a whirlwind of after-graduation-plans as well. Her future was shifting from the ideal in New York City, to the realistic in Kansas City. Both amazing opportunities, the first city had captured her heart though. Needless to say, it was a pretty mediocre week for succeeding at finding Contentment.

I asked my friend Sarah to pick the next word, ready to move on from my unmet challenge. It took her a couple days, but she came up with the perfect word: Contentment. She knew about my word the week prior and had also tried unsuccessfully to adopt it into her week. Dealing with a completely different realm of problems, she too was having trouble finding peace in the midst of chaos and joy in the midst of tribulations. Which is wisely why she acknowledged what I was so quick to shrug off: we both desperately needed Contentment. So together, Sarah and I carried on with this strange word. Paul's epistles speak so eloquently of his secret to finding contentment, and this was when he was in jail. So why were we struggling so much, two middle-class women who hadn't known a single day of animosity and true need?

The answer came in the form of a Timothy Keller podcast. Late for church one morning, I decided to stay home and listen to a podcast of a preacher that had great reviews from my college-community. The first that popped up was "Freedom in Contentment". Was it a simple coincidence? No, I like to acknowledge divine intervention when I find myself at the receiving end. As I mentioned before, I was humbled by the challenge of contentment. It wasn't because I hadn't mastered it the two weeks prior. It was because I unassumingly thought that I could. Pointed out so eloquently in his sermon, Keller reminded his audience that contentment was not a lesson, it was a journey. This was not a "word of the week" this was a "word of the lifetime".

An entire sermon was preached on a few simple verses found in Philippians. Verses 4:11-13 were thoroughly examined as they state, "I have learned in whatever situation I am to be content. I know how to be brought low, and I know how to abound. In any and every circumstance, I have learned the secret of facing plenty and hunger, abundance and need. I can do all things through him who strengthens me." Paul learned. He found out the secret. It wasn't something he found sitting on the side porch of his friend's home, though the journey may have started in a similar fashion. It was found in the depths of a jail cell, void of any earthly possession or security, yet still filled with peace, joy, and trust that God was still good and in control. Because the secret of Contentment, it turns out, is found at the end of dreams. If those dreams unravel and you find yourself with nothing, contentment sneaks in to save the day and confirm that God's love is all you could ever need. On the other hand, if those dreams come true, contentment saves the day in a completely different way. Instead, it points out that all you could achieve will never be enough to replace the necessity of God's love. And lucky for you, that Love is abundant.

Most of us teeter along the lines of plenty and want. It's going through times of prosperity and peril that reveal true contentment, however. It's these epic moments in your life story that shed light upon maturity. When you find yourself in pure happiness, whatever tangible form it presents you, acknowledge God still. Acknowledge that a puppy is such a joy, but it will not replace the joy of redemption. Acknowledge that a secure job in a high-rise overlooking the city is a beautiful blessing, but our job is to ultimately be beacons of Light for the lost. And if your plans become shaky and the tangible evidence of God's love is hard to come by, remember He is still there. He is holding up your foundation and hiding joys in new pockets of life for you to discover down the road.

It fills me with joy to know Contentment is a journey and not a destination. I have glimpses of it in my life already, but I know I'm not there yet. And I've decided that I want to be the best version of myself when I'm old and grey, and have weathered a few more storms. I know that's when my relationship with God will be the strongest and I can daily work towards that betterment. The first step on this journey is identifying the areas of your life that are robbing you of contentment. Is it the approval of others, making sure that their labels adequately reflect how you view your own self? Is it found in having your life perfectly align with your preconceived notions of how it should unfold? Whatever it is, acknowledge it. Be honest with yourself and really look at where your self-esteem and identity are derived from. If it is not Jesus Christ, then it shall surely crumble at some point. The rest of the journey is an ebb and flow, finding yourself in plenty and in want, and deciding what to do when you're presented with those situations. I hope you choose contentment, I hope you find joy, experience peace, and realize how safely you are held in the wings of our Savior.

Road Trips:

"Happiness is not a state to arrive at, but a manner of traveling."
— Margaret Lee Runback

When I was eight years old, our family embarked on a two week journey out West. The final destination was to visit San Diego, California to visit family, but the rest of the journey is held equally dear in my heart. That's because my parents made sure to make the manner of traveling every bit as part of the vacation as the destination was. Instead of flying over the mountains, we drove right on through them. Instead of mindlessly passing through cities, we stopped to indulge in their culture.

There is so much life between California and Kansas. So many roads travelled daily by hardworking people, and so many vastly different landscapes painting their daily life. We saw the Rocky Mountains in Colorado, the Sequoias in Northern California, and the Grand Canyon in Arizona. Needless to say, there were many moments that simply took my breath away. As a bonus, each landscape teemed with a unique culture. We ran into cowboys, hippies, Native Americans, and fellow vacationers. All of them had stories, and we were able to be part of them. Travelling at such a young age, I was quite impressionable and impacted in a very unique way. I caught the disease of Wanderlust, and the only known cure is Adventure.

The trip out West has been mimicked many times in my life, but they just go by slightly different labels. There was the road trip to see every major zoo in the Midwest. Then there was the road trip in a sixteen passenger van to New Orleans. One time there was a road trip with no true destination at all (you'll read about that later). But always, always, there have been the road trips to camp.

Perhaps one of my favorite camp road trips was heading down South to Camp War Eagle. I was a live-in counselor for a camp in Rogers, Arkansas and decided the five hour trip would be more fun with other passengers. I got set up with two girls I had never met before to make that trek. There's nothing like being stuck in a car to get to know each other! Luckily, they were two wonderful people, ones I would gladly hop back in a car with. I think it speaks volumes to how much travelling lets you put your guard down. Whether it's intentional quality time, or time that you stumble upon, road trip conversations seem to flow in a way owned only by the roads. Sometimes you get lost and have to point each other in the right direction. Sometimes you get a flat tire or the rain is pouring so hard you can't see, and you are forced to pull over to the side of the road and assess the situation. Road trips parallel life in this manner. We're all journeying together, searching for some destination, but haven't yet arrived. We have the joyous opportunity to join others and make memories simultaneously and reflect on them when the journey is over. Having others in the car with you ensures extra internal compasses to point you in the right direction (especially if yours is a little rusty).

Angels in Disguise:

I believe in angels. I believe that they are all around us, and sometimes, through divine intervention, they come into our lives and teach us valuable lessons. The passage Matthew 25:30-35 has always stuck out to me. It's here that Jesus says "I tell you the truth, whatever you did for the least of these, so also you did for me." This verse is what has guided my moral compass over the years. It's what is gently whispered when I see the lost, the broken, the helpless, and the innocent. I know I've had a few encounters with these angels, the least of these, and they have forever changed my heart.

When I lived in Arkansas, there was a homeless woman well known in the community. She was not known for her endearing quirkiness or ability to hold her own. Her reputation was that of a con-artist, someone who took advantage of charities and didn't think twice about the words she spoke. In a parking lot one evening, she approached a friend and me in a panic. She claimed her son was in the hospital and she needed money for a hotel room. She needed her hotel room because her father would be very upset if he found out she slept in a chair in a waiting room. Being poor college kids ourselves, it was a relief not having to lie about our lack of money, we simply didn't have any. So instead of turning her away and brushing her off, we offered her something else, friendship. People to experience life with for a few minutes. We were real with each other, we talked about our burdens, our joys, our hopes. And this homeless woman stopped looking so homeless and a lot more like myself. Though she had known many more hardships than I will ever fathom, she still had a great capacity for love and an even greater need to be loved. We sat in the parking lot and prayed, then hugged and parted our separate ways. I never saw her again, but I knew she was a little slice of Heaven in the most obscure of ways.

I also believe that children can be angels. Many times we consider them "the least of these". Most are unable to act independently of their family units, to form complex thoughts and impact the world greatly. But there are always a few who slip through these expectations and pursue greatness despite the adversity that faces them. While touring a half-way home for youth, I met a little boy that defied all of the expectations set before him. The home provided a loving environment for boys that were either taken out of their homes by concerned social workers or had chosen to be reformed rather than serve time in juvenile detention. A unique environment, I was impressed with the amount of beauty that had come from brokenness. The way that the parental models had taken the "least of these" and molded them into humble children of God. They saw the good in each child and made sure that they would have a spot of happiness in this season of their lives.

The boy that I met was truly a living picture of how our Savior creates beautiful things. Taken out of his home at a young age, he came to the house and lived there for two years. Sadly, he ran away, back into the arms of those he knew to be his flesh and blood. After being back in the home environment that he had been saved from years before, he saw the contrast of how much darkness still existed there. He knew if he stayed, that darkness would seep deep into the veins of his existence and if he didn't go back now, he may never make it out. So, he came back to the home on his own terms and is flourishing. We were able to bond over one overarching similarity: we love to write. Amidst the playful rambunctiousness of the house, I was lost in a book. This book was written by the boy and he wanted to get a fellow writer's feedback on it. It was phenomenal. I couldn't believe that it was written by a ten-year-old boy who had known so much brokenness already. Through the turn of each page I was able to see how therapeutic writing truly was for him, as his message turned from a cloud of darkness to that of hope. His message that he shared with me, I want to share with you also. Through all the dark nights, there are stars there to guide us, beacons of light shimmering to let us reach our destination safely. They may be physical lamps, or family members, friends, or maybe even guardian angels...

Skipability:

I should probably preface this section with the fact that I genuinely love to learn. Since I was little, I've always wanted to know more about my surroundings and the history of my species. I am a huge advocate for education and nurturing your brain, but I believe the mind and soul should be nurtured alongside. I've taken many courses throughout my student-hood. Some of them required my utmost attention, others refined my doodling skills. Within the first week of the semester, you can generally tell where your class fits along that spectrum. Some teachers require attendance, while others will post lectures on-line thanks to technology. My advice to you: respect the skipability of your classes.

There are just some days when you need to sleep in, make banana pancakes, go on a bike ride through City Park, and thank goodness for friends that volunteered to take notes on the lecture. I smile looking back on the memories I've made that wouldn't have been possible if I was sticking to my weekly routine. I suppose it's a bad habit that originated from misusing my press-pass in high school, but it's seen me to some much needed mental health breaks. The thing about skipping class is that it has to be done sparingly. The point of it is to break free from routine, not make it become part of your routine. That's where the magic lies. If it's interfering with your school work, or your job, or declining your test scores, then it ceases to be a positive experience. But a few times a year, it makes your day more special and more memorable, without the negative consequences of making it your life style.

My freshman year, I made a very wise decision to miss my Friday afternoon classes. It had been a long winter and the sun chose to peek through the clouds that day. It was probably sixty degrees, but it climbed to ninety in my memories. Emily and Sara were my accomplices and we decided a day at the lake was simply the only cure for the winter blues. So, we climbed in Sara's car, rolled down the windows, turned up the music and fled from responsibility for a few hours. The rest of the day was spent on the beach, taking pictures and taking in the sweetness of sunshine and friendship. I'm not sure what I missed in class that day, but I never would have wanted to miss out on one of my warmest memories of that season.

From the time I stepped foot in the classroom to today, when I'm about to step on stage and accept my diploma, scholastic expectations have changed drastically. It's a beautiful thing that education has become more accessible to those of all social and economic backgrounds. And it's a beautiful thing that courses have to evolve each year to keep up with scientific discoveries. But, along with this expansion of education has come the expansion of expectations. Elementary students are being prepared to be test takers first, learners second. College students are expected to become graduate students. Adults are given the chance to go back to school and get a completely new degree, all from the comfort of their own home. With the stress that accompanies these changes, I would be disappointed if it started to replace the joy of learning. So wherever you're at in particular in your studies, make sure you are still embracing the whimsy that education can offer. Take time to grab coffee with a friend during a study binge. Take time to watch clouds shift their form in the sky instead of going to your Geology 101 class. Those lessons will stick with you longer than thirty minutes of typical class will. Go on, embrace the skipability.

Marion, Kansas:

"Sometimes there are moments in life that are too profound for words."

On December 17th, 2013 I spent the day in Marion, Kansas. Though the quote from Emily Carnes above is true, I will try to find the right words to describe what happened in this city. After finals had culminated, we decided to take a road trip to a small town just to see what treasures we could discover. Little did we know, there were many interactions to take place that would forever change our lives.

Driving through the plains on an unusually warm winter afternoon, we made many pit-stops in search of the perfect place to spend the day. We stumbled through cities named Hope and Gypsum until we showed up on the doorstep of Marion. It was lunchtime when our adventure began, so we stepped into a pizza parlor. There was a group of women ranging from the ages of seventy to ninety just enjoying the afternoon with each other. Without hesitation, Emily and I joined their luncheon and soaked up wisdom from their old, beautiful souls. They shared stories about their families and encouraged us to keep cherishing our twenties. The advice they gave us was simple yet profound. They collectively agreed that the most important thing we can do right now is to be happy. That's it. Often times, at twenty-something, we feel this impulse to chase happiness and run down our dreams and forget that sometimes we just need to smile and acknowledge our blessings. They said to not grow up too fast, to treasure this time. They love the age they're at, being grandmothers and great-grandmothers. Nursing their husbands back to health after war, losing loved ones, raising children, all of these moments they've experienced were tough, but they were worth it. We'll have good days, and we'll have some bad. But if we hold onto the obtainable goal of happiness, we'll be just fine. We can find joy in the little things and they'll get us through the hard days. Be happy where you're at. Life flies by so quickly.

Continuing our adventure in Marion, we stumbled upon a few antique stores. What treasures we found there! The best treasure was not an item, no, it was a wonderful woman named Prudy. Her real name is Prudence, but her friends call her Prudy. The name is fitting for that spunky 84 year old and I'm glad we jumped to the status of friend that afternoon. Wandering around the store, Emily and I were stopped by Prudy when she asked if we were sisters. Flattered, we said no, we're just friends having a wonderful adventure together. At the moment, she was contemplating a purchase and thinking it over in a lazy-boy chair. So, we joined her and plopped onto chairs with her as well! For the next two hours, Prudy shared her story and gave us advice that had so much depth. It was one of those conversations that left you speechless because you just knew afterwards you'd never be the same.

She started off her story by explaining why the purchase she was about to make was so hard. She was trying to find the perfect cabinet for her family room since the old one needed to be replaced. Her carpenter husband had recently passed away, and though the cabinet she was interested in was fine, there was just no comparison to the ones he crafted during his prime days. She explained that this hard time in her life was such a blessing in disguise. Instead of mourning this emptiness left by him, she chose to celebrate her Beloved's life and rely on the strength of the Lord and her friends. Prudy emphasized that investing in others is one of the most important things you can do in this lifetime. We will have no idea the extent to which we will need to rely on others to help us through the hard times, but most importantly embrace the good times with. Her heart-level friends helped her through this time and showed her that friendship is everlasting and will bless you ten times over. Out of the blue, she looked both of us in the eyes and said "Girls, just don't worry. God's timing is perfect and He has a beautiful plan for you. I'm not sure where you're at in life, but if you're worried about who you're going to marry or where you're going to live, don't. He has it all taken care of and He loves you so much." Well, that was exactly what both of us needed to hear. While most of society verbalizes the need to be pieced together and presentable, she reminded us that it's okay to not have it all figured out. We don't need to chase after men or money or materials, because God provides. He delights in us and reveals His plan when He deems best.

The final bit of wisdom Prudy offered was to never lose hope. Always be on the lookout for miracles, because her life has been one. From the beginning, she was set up to fail. Born with a birth defect, she was near death and miraculously saved. In a bad marriage with two small children, she was delivered into a new family with a new and faithful husband who her children endearingly call "Daddy". Her Beloved late husband was a miracle in himself, showing the redemption that God so lovingly shows us. He too had his share of close calls, but his survival through them could only be attributed to miracles. When talking of traveling and vacationing, she wittily told us "Island hopping is over-rated. It's much better to immerse yourself where you travel and experience the beauty around you." Amen Prudy. Here's to being on the lookout for miracles and immersing ourselves fully wherever we may be at.

The journey home was just as lovely as the people of Marion. We stopped at a lake that had been frozen over by the breath of December. The whole lake was flocked with thousands of geese who were preparing to take flight down South. It's amazing how they know internally where they belong and how to go about getting there. The Harvest Moon was also in flight that evening. It was a warm yellow beam floating through the sky, protecting us and the rest of the Midwest with its guiding light. You never know the depth of your interactions with strangers. When presented with the opportunity to meet new friends, go for it. You may only speak for a few minutes, but your lives could both be changed for a lifetime. I know mine has been.

Mermaids:

"I must be a mermaid, for I have no fear of depth and great fears of shallow living." – Anais Nan

We all experience fear at some time or another. Heights, spiders, in-laws, clowns, past mistakes, the list of things people are afraid of goes on and on. But when these fears creep in, it is important to give them names instead of cowering away. Naming them not only drains their power, but it also allows you to see them in a new light. From a survival stand point, fear is good. It is the force that keeps us from leaning too far over the edge or walking barefoot through rubble. It's what gave our ancestors a healthy fear for predatory animals and in doing so kept them alive. In this light, fear is equivalent to respect. And that respect has the power to be used as a driving force, something to move you forward.

My fears range from season to season. When I was ten years old, I fainted at the doctor's office after an immunization. Needless to say, a phobia of needles was acquired. I wouldn't even have to be in a hospital or in view of a needle, if someone brought up that memory, I would clam up and start panicking. This eerie feeling would creep over me and all I could think of is how sharp objects should not be poked into my body. Thankfully, after some hospital exposure, and some occasional light headedness, I grew out of my phobia. But now, as I approach a new season on unknown, I am naming a new fear: failure.

This is the first year that failure has crept into my mind. It's not because I've never failed before, but it's because I have never stood so close to the edge of my plans. When I planned for this season of college, I knew (hoped) it would last four years. I knew that at the end of this season, I would surely start the other one, on some other cliff's edge. But now that I approach the end of my path, my fear is not of failures past or present, but of ones that could possibly decorate my future. I'm scared of the possibility that some may look at the mess of my life and name it as failure. Today, fear is a little larger than it was yesterday.

Certainly, this is a fear known by many, loathed by all. So, I had this idea. What if I gave this fear a name, called it by something else? What if I talked about it and didn't let it take up any more room in my brain; that same brain that is capable of imagination and creating dreams? What would that look like? Well, I'm learning that it looks pretty beautiful. Instead of running away from the possibility of failure, I'm greeting this fear like an old friend. A quirky friend that you maybe don't tell all your secrets to, but surely you sit down and have a good time together every once in a while. This friend has some advice: let fear be a driving force.

When fear of failure becomes a driving force, it looks inherently different. Instead of succumbing, I am now succeeding. And this is all done by a slight alteration of perspective. Walking hand in hand with this fear causes me to instead wander towards a reality where I am successful. It causes me to realize that snapshots of my life are not enough to tell my life story, the whole panorama is required. I may be working minimum wage, hiking through the mountains for cheap entertainment, but that is in no way a fail. In the future, I may still be a hired hand and somewhat directionless, but I know that I will be okay. Because not failing is more than succeeding, it's what you do with that success and do in those moments that you don't feel so important.

Me, I will take these fears and sprout new wings. I will continue to walk down my life path confidently and find happiness in even the most inconspicuous of places. I will trust that my interactions run deeper than I could ever fathom, and I cannot define my success by glancing at the surface. I will have no fear of this depth, but only entertain a great fear of shallow living. That's my story, what's yours? How will you turn things that scare you into things that dare you to be the best version of yourself?

Thin Places:

On the last night of camp, some fellow co-counselors brought quilts out to the soccer field to star-gaze. It was a crisp clear evening that allowed your eyes to focus on stars belonging to galaxies not yet named. Since it was the last night, and we were all from different colleges, we were all aware it may be our last conversation with one another. And if it wasn't the last, it certainly would be a while before our paths crossed; so we wanted to make sure our words were chosen carefully. Anything that had yet to be exchanged during the summer came to the surface. We wanted to make sure our stories forever affected that group lying on old fleece blankets and home-made quilts.

I learned a lot that evening, but more than simply increasing my knowledge, I became aware. Aware of what was going on around me, aware of how people's lives affect one another. And also aware of Thin Places, or so what my friend Brooke calls them. It's an old Irish legend actually, which puts a name to the feeling of being a little closer to Heaven. Places where you can almost grasp the intangible, places where you experience inexplicable peace, places that cause you to reflect upon who you are and where you want to be. The Celtic phrase quirkily states, "Heaven and earth are three feet apart, but in thin places that distance is even shorter."

We've all stumbled upon these places, and I hope this chapter conjures up some images of Thin Places past. They aren't places that you can go looking for, they're only found when you stumble upon them. Sometimes we just don't have our eyes or our hearts open enough to realize we're standing in them. And other times our thin places are so simple, like a neighborhood park, that we feel fickle associating any depth to them. They don't have to be considered great by all to have a huge impact on your life, often times they just sneak their way into it.

As we were stargazing and talking about Thin Places, I realized that most of my thin places, or thin moments, find me in a very similar state. My thin places are often lying on my back, looking at the sky, contemplating the shimmering specks that change like a kaleidoscope before my eyes. After a mission trip in New Orleans in high school, our youth group took a left turn and wound up in Galveston for a fun-filled day. A day of beach shenanigans slowly transformed into an evening of reflection and restoration as we headed to the pier for a devotional. A wanderer by nature, I found myself at the end of the pier star gazing while the rest of the youth group sang songs and talked about their weeks in Louisiana. There was not one cloud in that night sky and I took my spot at the end of the rocky pier to glimpse at the Lord's latest masterpiece. Waves crashing all around me, city lights and human voices in the far off distance, just me and the sky. In that moment, I could have sworn I was infinite. That pier was, however, infinitely thin.

Another star moment that called for jaw dropping, hands raised reverence, happened off the coast of Grand Cayman island. On a family vacation to the Caribbean, we decided to go on a Bioluminescence tour. It's a strange, seasonal phenomenon where bacteria in certain bays light up like the night sky at any sign of movement. I could have easily been convinced that we were actually on the movie set of Avatar, but real life always has a way of outshining the movies. The tour took us kayaking along the coast in the middle of the night with a glowing cove as our destination. At the swish of a fish's tale or the stroke of a paddle, the bacteria would acknowledge the presence of movement with a bright green glow. Overwhelmed with the beauty, I looked up to the sky to thank God for this beautiful gift. Upon glancing though, I caught a glimpse of a few shooting stars. Beauty overload.

Over the years, I've encountered so many more thin moments. They aren't ones that I intentionally search out by any means, but I am a lot more aware of the weight that they carry now. After learning about this Celtic explanation of that mysterious hope and joy inside, I can't help but notice how often I stumble upon them now. There are spots I take friends and family to around my city that I feel like I can almost see past the veil of uncertainty. And there are spots that have popped up unexpectedly on planned out journeys that have left me forever changed for the better. So keep your eyes open, you just might happen upon them yourself. One person's thin place can certainly vary from another's, but all leave us humbled and reminded of better places to come.

Draw Me Gently:

Draw me gently to my knees,
So I can see you Kings of Kings,
For I know,
I'm not alone.

Lord I pray You'll lead my steps,
To match the beat inside Your chest,
And I know,
They'll lead me Home.

And when it seems I've lost my way,
You shed Your light and cleanse with grace,
I oughta know,
You are my hope.

Breathtaking is Your beauty here,
I once was blind but now it's clear,
A daily show,
Creation flows.

Falling in Your divine sound,
Your music wraps me all around,
Symphonies grow,
You won't let go.

You have planted in me dreams,
Pouring out blessings in between,
Where You say go,
I'll always follow.

October:

"Don't frown because it's over, smile because it happened."
-Dr. Seuss

It's my last October living in Manhattan. I have so many mixed feelings about this. On one hand, I am lucky that I know it's the beginning of the lasts. This way it won't simply slip away unnoticed. I can acknowledge the fact that I am leaving, acknowledge the fact that like my life, the leaves are changing, and just because they are different colors does not make them any less beautiful. Instead of regret or longing, I can appreciate the beauty of this month and all the weight that it carries.

Ever since I can remember, October has been my favorite month. If my life was made up entirely of Octobers, I would be the happiest gal alive. The crisp air, the warm sweaters, reading books outside, bonfires, plaid, chai tea, piles of leaves; I am convinced that all things good and beautiful originate in the month of October. This October has been no different. Each day I walk around the city, I have to catch my breath because of the beauty. The leaves are such a brilliant kaleidoscope of colors, more vibrant than I could ever reproduce in a painting or even a photo.

Walking through campus today, I caught the scent of crunched up leaves and smiled as memory overpowered my senses. It brought me back to a bike ride on the paths as a child. Passing by the creek, I would always smell the most powerful aroma in the fall. Ecstatic about discovering the most beautiful of perfumes, I asked my parents what that scent could possibly be. They explained that it was simply crumpled up leaves, ones that had died and made their new home among the reeds by the riverbank. I thought to myself, how could this be? How could my favorite scent be caused by something as morbid as a deceased plant? But my parents explained the process of shedding leaves even further. The seasons were in a cycle, and in order for the new leaves to come again in spring, these leaves needed to fall and make room. The leaves wouldn't be able to survive winter, so instead of freezing in the cold, they twirled brightly to the ground in their autumnal dance voluntarily. And just like the Semisonic lyrics so wisely point out, "every new beginning comes from some other beginning's end", a new tree is able to blossom come spring time.

And just like my wish, the world around me is becoming more and more like October. The crisp wind may send shivers one day, but it always sends warm blankets and warm friends to compensate. While there are many distinct seasons from my past I wish I could hold on to, I know they could not hold their same beauty here in the present. They happened for a reason and part of their beauty lies in the fact that they didn't last forever. They were fleeting, and that made them special and gave them a hint of extra value. And just like the leaves have to make way for new blossoms, some seasons in life make way for the sweet blooms of springtimes yet to come.

Be Intentional:

As my time at K-State dwindles down, so do my days as a sorority girl. Towards the end of the year my sorority, like many others, has a senior week. It's a week dedicated to the oldest members who are heading off into the real world and replacing their active status to alumni. The week starts off with a night of advice from the seniors. The seniors share memories accumulated from within the walls of the sorority house, but also are given the opportunity to share the wisdom that was collected alongside those memories. A few days before, my mind flooded with all of the moments that had shaped my college-hood. I recalled road trips, date parties, and lounging on the side porch to name a few. I realized that all of my memories really just pointed towards one piece of advice: be intentional.

I've been blessed to have been exposed to this practice at a young age. I've had older friends speak truth into my life and reveal that people were always going to be the most important thing in my life. I'm sure I would have figured it out eventually, but it was nice to get that nudge in the right direction early on. To me, being intentional is defined as taking the time out of your day to make others a priority. It's about truly getting to know those around you whose paths somehow lined up perfectly with yours for the time being. Being intentional means delving past surface level with friendships and meeting each other with great depth.

During college, it can be so easy to look past being intentional. With so many outlets to get plugged into, camaraderie with many gets mistaken for a quality conversation with a few. Instead of relying on activities to bring you together, it is so important to seek each other out and pursue friendship. Even if it's just a thirty minute coffee break to find out about each other's week, that cup of coffee is still intentional.

Most of us live with an unacknowledged fear of getting to truly know people. Often, the root of this fear is striving for perfection. If people truly get to know you, they will also be befriending your struggles and secrets. The great thing about being intentional is that instead of living in fear of having the dark parts of your life show, you now have a friend to bring in light. Love covers over a multitude of wrongs, and you must let others in to experience this love. We must not float through life unscathed by others. Let others in. Let them know who you truly are, because most of the time they're quite similar. Imperfections and all.

Another reason for keeping each other at an arm's length is fear of detachment. Once you've let someone into your life, you expect them to be there for a long time, hopefully all of time. In some situations, this just can't be the case. There will be many seasons in your life that only last a week, or a month, or even just a day. As I met people in Ireland, I knew realistically I wouldn't be able to stay in contact with all of them. So when I arrived at the beginning of the summer, I knew I had a choice. I could act like I was only passing through and watch from afar, or I could really get to know the people that comprised that beautiful country. I'm so glad I chose the latter of the two; otherwise I wouldn't have accumulated so many stories and sweet memories. I also wouldn't have gotten to know Lola. Lola was an immigrant from South Africa whose path crossed mine multiple times in Ireland. I first met her at work, she was a physical therapy aide and I was a physical therapy intern. She had such a servant heart about her, so I shouldn't have been surprised when I saw her in a different pocket of life. A few weeks after being in the country, I found a church home on the other side of town. Lola had found the same church a few years earlier. She greeted me with open arms and ecstatically claimed me as her sister in Christ. She taught me many lessons, like how to find a home away from home, how to be respectful at work when you're serving those that may not deserve it, and how to be joyful in all situations. She didn't have a lot of earthly possessions, but she had a beautiful family and enough love to share with the entire country of Ireland. On my last day, there were no tears shed between us. She simply said, "Alright sister, I see you in Heaven." And that was that. And one day we shall meet again.

When she said that, I think I finally started to understand Matthew 6:20, "But store up for yourselves treasures in Heaven...for where your treasure is, there your heart will be also." These relationships that I've been harvesting, these people I've been intentional with, those are the only thing I get to take with me. There are so many daily distractions that are only temporary. Things like money, awards, jobs, all of which are noble and applause worthy. But at the end of the day, they are just extra "stuff", not treasure. As we grow in our friendships and choose people over items, that's when we start storing up our treasures. And what a beautiful thing to point our hearts back to their origin.

It's never too late to start being intentional. One of my friends approached me after I had given my bit of advice. She confessed that more than anything, my speech made her a little sad. She felt like she had chosen studying over friendships and made scholastic affairs her priorities. As she said it, I smiled, thinking of all of my memories I had with her. Well known for her brains, she is also well known for her gentle spirit and great leadership skills. She assumed that since she was succeeding at school, she wasn't succeeding in her friendships. That's when I realized that being intentional is not an "either or" type of practice. School does not have to be chosen instead of people, working hard at your job does not have to replace working hard at your marriage. Both can coincide quite nicely, it's simply a matter of realizing that people are more important. It's realizing that our time on earth is finite and we are so blessed to have others impact us for the better while we're here.

Letters:

At the turning of each year, I like to reflect. I reflect on how much has changed in 365 days; whether it's a change within me or the world around me. One way I gage this is by writing a letter to my future self. Each year, it differs slightly. Sometimes the letter contains a synopsis of my previous experiences, sometimes it's a request to live well and cherish each day of the upcoming year, and sometimes it just contains advice. At the turning of this year, I was happy to read a letter full of advice. Here's what was written...

"I hope you live a life you're proud of. If you find that you're not, I hope you have the courage to start all over again." – F. Scott Fitzgerald

Another year has come and gone, with it came love, laughter, and an ever changing, forever renewed outlook on life. As I enter this new year, lucky thirteen, I hope to bring with me all of the little moments I've collected; the memories that have molded who I am today. I hope this year continues to shape me into a better version of myself, full of grace and the wisdom that I'm not done learning or growing up. I still have so far to go and many adventures to be had. I hope this year finds me with new experiences, ones I could never even dream of. This is the year of Ireland, of finding myself when I am totally lost, making friends out of strangers, and letting God take the pen and write a few chapters (His are always my favorite!). This is the year of endings, it's bittersweet, but I'll be a senior in college. So I hope when I'm reading this a year from now, I will be living a life I am proud of. I know I'll stumble, I know I'll fall, I know I'll make mistakes and misread signs. But I pray that I stumble into the arms of my sweet Savior. And through all my mistakes and misinterpreted intuition, I pray that these seemingly insignificant events lead me to the life I'm supposed to live: one with passion, joy, and inexplicable peace.

That being said, always remember these things and try your best to live by them:

-One thing I've learned recently and hope I put into practice, is that God shouldn't be number one in my life. There shouldn't be a hierarchy of priorities separating God from my family, friends, self, and realms of life. He should be my all in all. In my relationships, in my studies and in whatever consumes my life.

-Always view the world with child-like wonder. Know at the heart of everyone lies someone searching for something to believe in. We're all fighting the same battles. Give someone an ally, not another enemy they need to shield out.

-You are a healer of the mind, body, and soul. God has entrusted you with many precious people. Remember that's what they are: fellow friends, not just nameless patients. Listen when people talk to you. Reflect, pray, look within. The right answers will be revealed when necessary.

-Stop running away. After twenty-one years you're getting pretty good at leaving sticky situations. Blame it on wanderlust, blame it on restlessness, blame it on what you will. Please learn how to harness this energy. Run towards something beautiful. Let yourself fall, God will catch you, I promise. Let yourself learn new things from an old place. Some answers are lying right in front of you. Dig deep.

-And hopefully this doesn't contradict the prior statement (I believe the two can coincide quite nicely!) but...never lose your sense of adventure. Never back down from an opportunity to go somewhere new or explore with friends. See great sites, climb great heights, go!! Let your vagabond soul search out the loveliest of places. Sleep under that magical blanket of stars. Remember how small you are and how big our God is.

-Indulge in your passions. Go running, drink coffee, read some novels, paint a picture, dance, go to a concert, frolic in the grass, catch fireflies, bake some sweets, play with puppies, swim in the ocean, sing to our Savior, learn from those much wiser, help others, swing on swings, do yoga, curl up with a cozy blanket, pick some wildflowers, go hiking and biking and kayaking, Your passions make you, you. They make you much muchier, never lose your muchiness.

-Live in peace. Try your best to get along with others and make them at ease. World peace will never be achieved without changing yourself first. Always be at peace knowing God is in control. He will never leave or forsake you, so never, ever, sweat the small stuff. Please.

-Be intentional. In all relationships, family, friends, acquaintances, know that every interaction has meaning. A simple hello, or long talk over tea, they all matter. People come into our lives for a reason, and vice versa. Whether it's for just a short time or a life time, we will only know in retrospect. But we can't live our life backwards. So always be intentional, you never know who could really need a friend, or who really needs to go on a road trip with you. It's both the little and the big things. Inspire people to be better versions of themselves, happier, healthier, filled with a bit more love each day. And don't for a second think you're better than someone (I know you won't but just a gentle reminder!). You're human, thus you're made of the same material.

-Never lose faith. God's timing is perfect. Don't give up when you can't feel Him, He's there and He is good. His plans for you are so much more beautiful than you could ever dream up for yourself. Enjoy the events the Lord dreamed up for you as they unfold before you. But for now, patience is key. It'll be worth it, I promise.

-Grow. Learn new things, soak up wisdom.

I can hardly wait to see what 2013 has in store. I don't know where I'm going, who I'll meet and what decisions I'll get to make. I don't know how many cups of coffee I'll drink, how many times I'll dance, how much sleep I'll get, or how different I'll be on 12-31-13. But I do know this: I will live it up. I will not waste this precious life I've been given. Here's to a new year, unwritten and full of many wonderful days to come.

Mentors:

"You were born with the ability to change someone's life, don't ever waste it."

When you hear the word "mentor", what images come to mind? Perhaps you think of a famous leader that has influenced you from afar. Maybe you think a mentor is somewhat of a prophet, untouched and unscathed by the ways of the world. Maybe they're perfect, maybe they're wise, perhaps a natural born leader. The title "mentor" has taken on compelling weight in today's society. It carries an amount of respect that no mentor feels they deserve or mentee feels they are able to deliver. But a mentor doesn't need to be an unachievable title that only belongs in old kung-fu movies and societal hierarchies. Mentoring can be as simple as pouring into someone or being the one receiving that information. It does not call for perfection or valiant achievements; all it calls for is being willing to be raw with one another. It calls for sharing your story and hoping that lessons can be obtained through the decisions you've made.

In order to experience growth to its fullest, it's important that you play three different roles in mentorship. There are times, if not now, in the future, where you need to be a mentor. This is the time to pass down what you've accumulated to someone who will be walking a similar path. You must also be a mentee to someone else. Choose someone older and wiser and simply soak up their wisdom. And the third role is that of a lateral mentor. Those are the heart-level friends that come along and grow with you side by side.

Mentor:
Outside of my family, there have been two women who have greatly poured into my life. I met my first mentor when I was eleven. Jenny Cox was my Sunday school teacher during fifth and sixth grade, but quickly became a dear friend. As their family expanded, our

friendship continued to grow as I became their nanny during high school. Before I was old enough to drive, Jenny would drive me to and from babysitting and share her life story with me. Drive by drive, we got to know each other better. Year by year, our friendship deepened. Like the best mentor/mentee relationships, it grew out of friendship. There was no document signing or commitment ceremony marking her decision to teach me unconditionally. There was simply a woman bursting with life experience, and a girl eager to create some of those memories for her own self someday. There are many little lessons Jenny taught me, but the importance of family was always the backbone of the lesson. She taught me how to discipline her children with love and logic, which in turn showed me how to interact with everyone around me. We all have the potential to grow. Jenny taught me how to gently awaken the desire to grow within those around me and to trust that your interactions always run deeper than you can fathom.

My other mentor is someone that has laid a solid path for me to follow. Taylor Penrod is three years older and about thirty years wiser than I am. We grew up together and our friendship has taken on many different shapes and forms throughout the years. During high school, I knew I could turn to her for unfiltered advice that sometimes just isn't available from those in a different generation. Taylor has been such a blessing because of her ability to see my footsteps faltering and immediately know how to bring me back to the right path. We've cried through mistakes and laughed through the bountiful blessings that have come our way. I've been shown firsthand how to let God's grace and power come into your life when you feel weak. I've been shown that material goods will never offer as much comfort as the security of God's unshakeable love.

Mentee:
Sarah Lewis is one of a kind. She is passionately driven and finds success wherever she plants her footsteps. I've sought discernment from her many times in my life, because even though she is a couple years younger, she operates at a much older level. That's why, when

she approached me about mentoring her this year, I was a little shocked. Though I was flattered, my mind also flooded with reasons why I shouldn't mentor her. I thought to myself, "I've made too many mistakes; I wasn't as strong of Christian when I was her age; I am not the wisest among her older friends." But then I realized something pretty cool, what Sarah needed was indeed someone who has made mistakes. What she needed wasn't perfection or the best of the best, she needed someone who was simply human and would help her grow as a human too. I realized that the stories I had to offer and the wisdom I had to pour out were enough to help her grow. So my advice to you is to never hold back when someone wants to get to know you better. You have a story written on your heart as well, and with a little guidance from God, you can share that with others and let them be changed for the better from it.

Lateral:
The lateral mentors in your life will be some of the most important people that you meet. Not because they will impart any more knowledge than older mentors, or because they will call you to be a better version of yourself than a mentee could. No, they are so vital because they are those you are in direct community with. They are your heart-level friends that grow onward and upward with you. A lateral mentor will give you advice one day and soak up wisdom from you the next day. There will be seasons where you may be pouring in or receiving more, but for the most part lateral mentors are simply the ones you do life with.

In life, when problems arise, we must first run to God. But He has a lovely way of answering our tough times by sending words of encouragement and strength through our lateral mentors. This is His way of sending tangible evidence that He is working all things together for the good of those who love Him. In each season I've found myself in, there have always been the wisest of lateral mentors. I've been able to gain perspective and passion from those around me. At a crossroads this year, my lateral mentor Emily Carnes had some astounding perspective. Her guidance has always been simple yet profound, and this advice was no different. On a road trip to Dallas she gently said, "In the scheme of things, our time on earth is so finite. We'll live no more than one hundred years here compared to our eternity in Heaven. As long as you're pursuing your God ordained passions, investing well in those around you, and not letting your talents lie dormant, you're doing it right and you're going to be just fine. There isn't a wrong place to be. In each scenario you'll experience some form of bliss. So why not follow your dreams? Why not live life out loud?"

Dreams:

"Don't let your dreams be dreams."

-Jack Johnson

Boldly written across my bedroom wall, the words above provide a daily challenge for me. I wake up each morning and see this call to action, and let it appropriately alter my footsteps for the day. As a dreamer, it's easy for me to conjure up grand plans and images of life experiences yet to come. While my imaginative side is usually an asset, it can sometimes be a danger. I can get caught up in the longing of a dream that I forget to implement it and see it through to culmination. That's why I needed Jack Johnson's lyrics to gently remind me of the most important part of dreaming: laboring those dreams into reality.

Thus far, my senior year of college has required much introspection. I've had to stop the task at hand to do some soul searching on numerous occasions. And when searching my life, I've continually been looking at my dreams. I look at dreams especially, because I think they play a much larger role than we give them credit for. Each day, we are presented with a series of choices, and I've found that I tend to make a lot of those choices based upon whether or not they will protect my dreams. It may be a simple dream, like to rent my own apartment. With that in mind, my daily choices begin to reflect this as I'm more cautious with my spending habits. And some dreams are bigger and broader, like my dream to be a source of hope and inspiration to others. With this dream in mind, I am more careful about what I say and who I surround myself with. Dreams can even impact your life without ever transpiring. They do this because they still end up altering routes that you take to get to your destination.

When presented with the opportunity to move to a big city with an even bigger heart, I felt myself wavering between my reality and dreams. The reality of the situation was that I would lack stability and assurance if I took a leap of faith and moved. The dream, it was to take that instability and root my faith even deeper. I began to ponder and ask myself, as a dreamer, would I be turning on my beliefs if I didn't in fact pursue my dreams? Since I am always encouraging others to take leaps of faith in their own lives, I knew my words would decline in value if they didn't match my actions. So I again turned to my wall to study those sweet lyrics.

I discovered that maybe, just maybe, Jack Johnson was on to something there. It could simply be that not pursuing dreams could leave you with a life full of regret. Maybe it's the kind that only hits a few times, at your child's graduation, on your fiftieth birthday, in the retirement home, someday, somewhere. But what if it's more than that? Could it be that this is an entirely different plane of existence that not many people tap in to? What happens when you really follow your dreams and see them through to existence? Maybe Jack knows that that's when all the greatness begins, and he's just letting us all in on his secret. A man playing guitar on the beach and getting paid for it...I think he might possibly be a genius.

This year has turned from merely conjuring up colors, to getting those hues onto a canvas. It's been a year of planning road trips, and heading out into wide open spaces. It's been a season of intentional living and making sure that I'm *doing* as much as I'm *dreaming*. I've thoroughly enjoyed blending my hopes and dreams together with reality; they've turned out to complement each other quite nicely. So my advice, whatever season of life you find yourself in, is to pay attention to your dreams. Pay attention to them, for they are love letters from God. They serve as both a map and a compass for where you are and where you want to be. Who knows what great things lie in wait at the culmination of those dreams.

The Meaning of Life:

As this little book of mine concludes, I want to leave you with this resounding question: what is the meaning of life? Just because it is a weighty question, does not mean it doesn't require an answer. I think that we all have a little piece of the answer within us. If you ask a stranger on the street, they may reply with something vague, possibly sarcastic. According to them, life could be about indulging in your passions. Maybe they think it's just a waiting place and the greatness begins as our chapters end. There are as many answers as there are inhabitants of this earth.

I've found that if you want answers, just ask the questions. So, I asked some people around me what they thought the meaning was. Their answers were beautiful reflections of who they are and how they choose to live their lives. My friend Jillian, a living example of love, matched her answer to her lifestyle. She is always seeking to serve others, whether it is at work, on a mission trip, or in class, she lives a life of service. Her response, "I would say it's discovering God's purpose for your life which will lead you to fully become your true self. You can do this by using your God given talents as a gift to others."

Wondering if I inherited my definition, I asked my dad what he thought the meaning of life was. His was similar to Jillian's answer. He said, "We were created to be in relationship with God. So to me the meaning of life is to do what you can to maintain and enhance that relationship. That underlying principle manifests itself in all other activities such as work, ethics, caring for others, relationships with others, etc."

An old roommate and dear friend of mine, Keagan, saw that each person's meaning may differ from another's. Her answer reflected her passion for individualism and the beauty that can come from embracing the unique and unordinary. She said, "Day to day I find 'life's meaning' simpler yet bolder than before. It is different from person to person. We each must realize what is written specifically on our soul, this is our personal 'meaning'. No one else can tell us. Clues are found in natural interests, talents, and convictions. We have the choice to seek out this powerful meaning we've been entrusted with." The complexity of her answer was contrasted with our other roommate's simple answer. Serena said the meaning of life is to, "Love others."

Many others answered with similar themes. This was an enjoyable chapter to write. It gave me a glimpse into the driving forces of my friends and family. I smiled at each response because each person was living out their definition. So here's what I think: even if your definition varies from the ones listed above, it's still right. It's right because you make it real when you live it out. God sets us all out on different paths and whispers compelling instructions to each one of us. Take some time to be still and find out what your answer is. Really, what is the meaning of life?

I've reflected on this throughout the years, and my own definition has slowly transformed into what I feel today. I know we're here for a purpose. We are here to be beacons of Light for one another. That's my own personal answer. I think that the relationships we harvest, the strangers we encounter, the person driving in the car in front of you, we're all here to help each other out. It can be a dark, scary place out there. There are times when none of this makes sense, when we're bombarded with news of missing planes and school shootings. This world is not our home, and you'll be reminded of it about ten times a day. That's why is so important that we shine our lights for one another. To shed light onto each other's paths and hold hands when we're lost or scared. We're all just walking each other home, and I certainly like my companions.

Conclusion:

This book is a simple collection of my thoughts on life. It started out as a letter to a friend and just kept growing. I hope that the words on these pages have met you where you're at and invited you to be a better version of yourself. We were not created to be stagnant creatures, but beautiful souls ever growing and shifting. I pray that you often stop and ask yourself who you are and where you want to be. And I pray that any and every season you find yourself in offers some sort of insight into your purpose and calling.

I hope through these pages you've been able to see that life is made up of times of great magnitude as well as miniscule moments. Sometimes you'll be living out your wildest dreams, other times you'll be conjuring up the next wild escapade. Life's about the journeys that bond you with friends. Life's about the times you can't fall asleep because you'd rather stay up and catch the sunrise. These are the memories you conjure up when you recall stories and mark down milestones. But life's also about the little things, the little moments. Pay attention to your surroundings when you feel like you're in-between dreams. So much life still happens, even if it doesn't feel noteworthy or important. Enjoy the little things, as Ben Rector once sang, "Because it's not the mountain tops, it's the walking in between."

Cheers.